INTEGRATIONIST
NOTES AND PAPERS
2014

Integrationist Notes and Papers 2014

Roy Harris

Emeritus Professor of General Linguistics in the
University of Oxford

Visit us online at www.authorsonline.co.uk

A Bright Pen Book

Copyright © Roy Harris 2014

Cover design © Laura Harris

British Library Cataloguing Publication Data.
A catalogue record for this book is available from the British Library.

ISBN 978-0-7552-1613-0

Authors OnLine Ltd
19 The Cinques
Gamlingay, Sandy
Bedfordshire SG19 3NU
England

This book is also available in e-book format, details of which are available at HYPERLINK "http://www.authorsonline.co.uk"

Contents

Preface

This volume of Integrationist Notes and Papers brings the number of items published in the series to a total of 60. The author would like to thank all those who commented on earlier versions, to Rita Harris for her excellent editorial work, and to Laura Harris for designing the cover.

R.H.
Oxford, January 2014

52

On Agreement

Agreeing with someone else seems to be a simple everyday notion that everyone can readily understand. Agreement, we think, comes PDFin various degrees. You can agree with what your next door neighbour says 'entirely', or 'mostly', or 'up to a point'. You can agree 'provisionally' or 'on certain conditions' or even 'reluctantly'. None of this involves giving the notion of agreement any serious philosophical work to do. And perhaps that is just as well. It is too useful a notion to be thus burdened.

An example of 'serious philosophical work' is Wittgenstein's contention in *Philosophical Investigations*: 'If language is to be a means of communication there must be agreement not only in definitions but also (queer as this may sound) in judgments' (Wittgenstein 2001: §242). The same thesis is repeated in his *Remarks on the Foundations of Mathematics*: 'We say that, in order to communicate, people must agree with one another about the meanings of words. But the criterion for this agreement is not just agreement with reference to definitions – but *also* an agreement in judgments. It is essential for communication that we agree in a large number of judgments.' (Wittgenstein 1978: 343).

He warns us: 'If there did not exist an agreement in what we call 'red', etc. etc., language would stop.' Since language shows no sign of stopping, we are invited to conclude that such agreements do indeed exist, and must be regularly continued, confirmed and extended. If there is to be communication about new techniques and new products, they too must be incorporated into our existing body of agreements.

But Wittgenstein sees that simply invoking the notion of agreement is not a definitive answer to the language problem. Potentially it opens the door to an infinite regress. He goes on to ask, 'But what about the agreement in what we call 'agreement'?' (Wittgenstein 1978: 196). He might have added: 'And how about the agreement in *that*?'. He concludes: 'It could be said: that science would not function if we did not agree regarding the idea of agreement' (Wittgenstein 1978: 197). Nor, one might say, would many other things, including elementary arithmetic. If there were no agreement that $2 + 2 = 4$ it is difficult to see how our everyday financial transactions, our buying and selling, could proceed, without an alternative agreement (e.g. $2 + 2 = 5$). The alternative to an arithmetic agreement would be *ad hoc* barter. Even if we were reduced to that, there would have to be a local agreement between A and B that what A is offering is acceptable in return for what B is offering, and vice versa.

Behind Wittgenstein's uneasy focus on the concept of agreement an integrationist will detect a reaction to the long-standing 'language myth' of the Western tradition; in particular, to the idea that communication between individuals is a process of telementation, or thought-transference. For B fully to understand what A says, it must be possible for B to interpret A's utterance as conveying exactly the thought which prompted A to utter it. Wittgenstein's contribution to the problem is to construe telementation not as some mysterious process of mental transference across the physical gap between A and B, but as a prior agreement between A and B on the relevant definitions and judgments. More exactly, Wittgenstein *replaces* the notion of telementation by that of interpersonal agreement.

It is the generalization of interpersonal agreement that introduces the notion of a linguistic community. There is no *private* agreement between A and B that they will use words in such-and-such ways. Linguistic communities are founded on the availability of *public* and freely accepted agreement about pronunciations, words and constructions.

In the light of Wittgenstein's commitment to this notion, it is interesting to see how other philosophers avoid the problem of agreement. Bertrand Russell's evasion is blatant. He merely says:

> I think that, in fundamental problems of language, its social aspect should be ignored, and a man should always be supposed to be speaking to himself – or, what comes to the same thing, to a man whose language is precisely identical with his own. This eliminates the problem of 'correctness'. What remains – if a man is to be able to interpret notes written by himself on previous occasions – is constancy in his own use of words: we must suppose that he uses the same language today as he used yesterday. In fact, the whole residuum of what was to have been done by the concept of 'correctness' is this: speaker and hearer (or writer and reader) must use the same language, i.e. have the same interpretative habits. (Russell 1940: 177-8)

To Russell's account the obvious objection is that if one is claiming to discuss 'the fundamental problems of language' one could hardly find a more fundamental problem than explaining how one person manages to understand what another says. To posit *ab initio* that they speak the same language is to take the language myth as gospel truth.

Russell admits that 'when I say 'there is a red flower' I expect others to see it too' (Russell 1940: 195). This is to assume a double agreement between Russell and others: (i) regarding the meaning of the words *there is a red flower*, and (ii) as to what *everyone* with normal eyesight can see.

*   *   *

In a linguistic community, are we all parties to the same agreement? If so, can we be certain exactly what the agreement is? Wittgenstein considers the case of going over a calculation several times to make sure there is no mistake. 'The danger here, I believe, is one of giving a justification of our procedure where there is no such thing as a justification and we ought simply to have said: *that's how we do it'* (Wittgenstein 1978: 199. Italics in the original.) This observation seems to suggest that there is no question of checking up on – verifying – the reliability of our habits, i.e. our customary ways of bringing about X by doing Y. The assumption is that unless our habits *were* reliable, we would long ago have abandoned them for more effective ones.

An integrationist will say that there is an important difference between doing something habitually and recognizing *that it is a habit*. We can, after all, reform our habits. We can give up smoking, drinking alcohol, having eggs and bacon for breakfast, and so on. Could we renounce *all* habits? If Wittgenstein is right, to renounce our *linguistic* habits would be to renounce verbal communication altogether, i.e. to give up on language.

'When somebody makes an experiment repeatedly 'always with the same result', has he at the same time made an experiment which tells him *what* he will call 'the same result', i.e. how he uses the word "the same"?' (Wittgenstein 1978: 199. Italics in the original.) The integrationist answer to this is 'No'. There is no experiment we can make to *discover* how we apply the concept of sameness. All we can do is reflect on cases where we are satisfied that two things are the same. Sameness is one of the concepts intrinsic to our integrational activities. Even when we cannot decide whether two things are the same or not, we are still looking for respects in which they *might* be. But this is not to say that we have an invariable concept of sameness that fits all cases. Sameness is always relative to the respects in which two or more things are being compared. 'Same weight' and 'same height' are incommensurables. They are not different dimensions of a common comparison.

Wittgenstein says: 'The word "agreement" and the word "rule" are related to one another, they are cousins. If I teach anyone the use of the one word, he learns the use of the other with it.' (Wittgenstein 2001: §224). This is perhaps the least convincing of all Wittgenstein's contentions about agreement. Many agreements that we recognize have nothing to do with rules (e.g. agreeing with others that it is too wet to carry on playing, or agreeing with others that John should have been here by now). For there is no *rule* about suitable conditions for play; or about John's punctuality either. There are simply individual judgments about these matters, and such judgments may or may not coincide. Someone who says, against the majority opinion, 'I think we should carry on playing' is not guilty of any infringement of what has been agreed. He merely differs from his colleagues, as he has every right to do.

* * *

'If you measure a table with a yardstick, are you also measuring the yardstick? If you are measuring the yardstick, then you cannot be measuring the table at the same time.' (Wittgenstein 1978: 199). But why not? It only sounds odd to talk about measuring the yardstick because we do not habitually use tables as standards of measurement. Measurement is always a *comparison*. We do not have standard tables, whereas we do have standard yardsticks. But if we did have standard tables, there would be no reason for refusing to accept 'This room is three tables long' as a measurement.

From an integrationist perspective, there is no such agreement as a *general* agreement about 'agreement'. I may agree with you that the weather is disappointing for this time of year. But this has nothing at all to do with my agreeing with you that $2+2 = 4$. Various kinds of agreement apply to various types of case. It is not important that we first agree to agree: what matters is that our actions (including our calculations) give results that in practice cause no problems in dealing with other people.

In resorting to the nebulous psychological notion of agreement Wittgenstein evidently fails to see that it has no explanatory role to play once we accept that mutually beneficial integration of activities – or anticipation of such benefit – is all that is needed to explain the many forms of human cooperation.

* * *

Can linguistic agreement be *imposed* on a population? This appears to be the idea behind the use that linguistic theorists make of the terms *standard* and *standardization*. Haas writes:

> The inherent variability of language would be a threat to communication if it were not held in check by an equally inherent normative tendency to maintain rule-governed standards of usage. Without the former, language would lose its adaptability to changing conditions; without the latter it would disintegrate. (Haas 1982: 19)

Here we see clearly what is misleading about discussing these issues as if they were properties of *language*. It falls not to language but to *language-users* to decide whether or not innovation is called for. And that will depend on particular circumstances. Most language-users are brought up to speak and write a traditional form of the language dominant in the country where they live. But they accept innovations if these are current among their contemporaries. The usual motivation for this acceptance is a reluctance to be seen as 'old-fashioned' or 'out of touch' with the times. It is the same motivation that shapes their tastes in clothes, food and recreational pastimes. There is nothing particularly 'linguistic' about it.

It is difficult to make sense of Haas's claim that without rule-governed standards of usage language would 'disintegrate'. Language will never 'disintegrate' as long as speakers and writers think it important to persuade, convince, or impress their addressees. Linguistic rules are nothing but the constructs of teachers, and their purpose is pedagogic. Such rules feature in school examinations, where they are identified with the notion of 'correctness'. But the idea that incorrect usage threatens communication or makes it impossible is a pedagogic shibboleth. Many if not most of the usages nowadays treated as 'standard' were originally condemned as 'incorrect' by conservative grammarians.

*   *   *

What kind of agreement with others is necessary in order to make sense of the world in which we all live? One obvious candidate is agreement about time. Without that we could never keep appointments. In fact, it would be pointless to make them. To cope with appointments, we need a common calendar and a common system of hours and minutes. But how accurate does this have to be? According to Russell,

> All science uses concepts which are in theory precise, but in practice more or less vague. 'One metre' was defined with all possible care by the French Revolutionary Government: it was the distance between two marks on a certain rod at a certain temperature. But there were two difficulties: the marks were not points, and temperatures cannot be determined exactly. (Russell 1940: 98)

Something similar applies to time, in Russell's view. When did the 19th century end? It is said to have ended at midnight GMT on 31 December 1900. But Russell notes:

> Midnight can only be determined by observations, say of chronometers; but no observation is exact, i.e., there is a finite period of time during which any given chronometer will *seem* to point to midnight; and, moreover, no chronometer is exactly right. Therefore no one could know exactly when the nineteenth century ended. Two views may be taken of this situation: first, that there was an exact instant when the century ended; second, that exactness is illusory, and that precise dating is even conceptually impossible. (Russell 1940: 98)

Integrationists will say that there is a third view; namely, that exactness sets a theoretical target for approximations in the integration of human activities. The time we live in is a 'more-or-less time'. Man-made clocks, watches and calendars are accurate enough for our everyday purposes. To demand more preciseness than these instruments provide is to take up residence in a philosophical cloud-cuckoo-land.

53

On Language Acquisition

Language acquisition has been called a 'miracle' (Fromkin and Rodman 1974: 188). It is certainly a topic which has attracted more than its fair share of miraculous explanations. Here is one:

> Linguistic practice is governed by a highly complex set of rules, even though the rules are rarely articulated; small children just pick them up at a colossal rate, learning to obey them without realizing that that is what they are doing. (Lycan 2008: 77)

The last sentence is ambiguous. Does this mean that children fail to realize *that these are rules*? Or does it mean that they fail to realize *that they have learnt them*? If both, here we have the miraculous attribution to children of an innate, subconscious capacity, i.e. the ability to recognize and follow linguistic rules before they have either encountered or detected any. And before they have had the chance to have anyone explain to them what a rule is.

Integrationists would be reluctant to entrust that explanation to Lycan, or any like-minded linguistic theorist who identifies languages with systems of rules. In 1968 Chomsky wrote: 'Only the most preliminary and tentative hypotheses can be offered concerning the nature of language, its use, and its acquisition' (Chomsky 1968: 23). This did not prevent him from assuming that linguistic behaviour is rule-governed, or from going as far as to postulate the existence of a specific 'Language Acquisition Device', presumably instantiated in some unknown neurophysiological form in the infant brain. It is worth noting that he did not postulate at the same time – even *en passant* – a 'Standing-Upright Acquisition Device', or a 'Bipedal-Gait Acquisition Device', although these would have been just as plausible, given that most children who survive to maturity eventually learn to do these things. (Perhaps he thought that standing upright and walking on two legs were not rule-governed activities.) The indication seems to be in any case that Chomsky thought that *linguistic* rules had a special status among the many rules that human beings may come to accept. He never seems to have realized that conjuring up innate devices for learning rules is just a pretentious way of making ignorance sound like science.

According to Chomsky, 'we have little reason to believe that behavior is "caused" in any well-understood sense of this term' (Chomsky 1986: 274-5). But that is precisely what we do have reason to believe when following a rule, i.e. we consciously *make* our behaviour conform to the rule's requirements, when it might not otherwise do so. This is as well understood a sense of the verb *cause* as we are likely to have need of. (Just as well understood as in *The rain caused him to run for shelter* or *The pain caused her to cry out.*) Making an insoluble enigma out of causation does not just preclude linguistics but eradicates science *tout court*.

Appealing to innate capacities has become the counterpart of appealing to divinities in former times. It requires no empirical evidence and nowadays it smacks of pseudo-science. Musicians do not explain learning to play the piano by postulating an innate capacity for piano-playing. Gardeners do not explain learning to mow the grass by reference to an innate capacity for grass-mowing. Just as a convenient divinity could always be found to preside over the rain, the river, the crops, etc., so an innate capacity can always be postulated for any human ability. Nothing could be easier. That is why postulating an innate capacity is the weakest of all explanations.
Unfortunately, like the gods of former times, innate capacities serve merely to divert attention from the serious study of how such abilities develop, quite apart from shrouding them in a kind of ontological mystery for good measure.

Here is a related example:

> If someone is riding a bicycle and falls off, that doesn't mean she does not know how to ride the bicycle...She might not be able to tell you the physical laws she is obeying to maintain her balance, but she knows how to ride the bike. Similarly, you may not be able to state the linguistic "laws" (rules) which account for your knowledge, but these rules make it possible for you to produce and understand an unlimited number of unfamiliar utterances...rules that you know without knowing that you do.' (Fromkin and Rodman 1974: 9)

This latter quotation exemplifies a widespread tendency among linguistic theorists to assimilate the acquisition of linguistic knowledge to learning about the physical world. For that is the most plausible analogue they can find of how to get by – and succeed tolerably well – without really understanding very much about it. Classical thermodynamics has laws we can feel the effects of, even when we are not aware that they have these effects, and cannot state the laws in question. But if Fromkin and Rodman's girl keeps falling off her bike, there comes a point where we have to ask whether she *has* learnt 'how to ride it'. Perhaps she has seen other people riding bikes and thinks that you just have to sit on the saddle with your feet on the pedals. Could it be that she knows how to ride it, but never manages to? It seems unlikely. Is it even a possibility?

Those scientists who believe that human behaviour is determined by laws of nature often concede that the outcome may be determined in particular cases 'in such a complicated way and with so many variables as to make it impossible in practice to predict' (Hawking and Mlodinow 2010: 32). What is evident in the case of the girl on the bike is our reluctance to admit unpredictable outcomes without convincing evidence. We prefer to say that she did not know how to ride, rather than that, although she did know, she kept on falling off for some unknown reason.

Theorists who appeal to the existence of rules to explain forms of learning often leave us in doubt about what they think a rule is. This is hardly surprising, because they always take care to characterize rules in terms of alleged results, never in terms of their actual operation. According to Foley and Thompson (2003: 3), 'all languages and all forms, be they spoken, written, electronic, and so on, are governed by rules of use and it is by adhering to these that effective communication is achieved.' Here 'effective communication' is proposed as the alleged result of rule-following. Since the authors of this sweeping claim presumably have no wider experience of language and communication than the rest of us, it is difficult to see how they can regard it as a universal truth empirically established. (How was it established, and by whom? Galileo? Newton? Einstein?)

The alternative would be to regard it as an ideal to be aimed at, albeit rarely achieved. It seems that Foley and Thompson are unsure which position to adopt. They tell us that linguistic knowledge is 'intuitive knowledge', and intuitive knowledge is 'deep-seated knowledge of something which has been learnt but which the learner cannot recall having learnt'. In short, they think the learning experience itself has been forgotten. The forgetting is what makes it 'intuitive'. Our defective memories are to blame.

This will not do. For one thing, it is difficult to reconcile with the notion that language-learning is a continuous lifelong process. Vocabulary recently acquired when we take up the study of a new subject, or unfamiliar words that we read in today's newspaper, are certainly not linguistic items beyond recall. We can often remember very precisely when and where we first met them.

Then again, no one would say that I have an 'intuitive' knowledge of Bill Smith's address if all that means is that I have forgotten when he first told me where he lived. Intuition is taken to mean something more impressive than forgetfulness.

Misconceptions about 'forgetting' our language-learning often go hand-in-hand with another confusion, also exemplified by

Foley and Thompson. This is the confusion between *languages* and *language*. 'Language', according to Foley and Thompson, 'is first and foremost a highly structured, rule governed, linguistic system.' But, in spite of their categorical assertion, language is nothing of the kind. Sport (as distinct from particular sports) is not a system. There are no rules of sport as such. *John has learnt to play sport* (as opposed to *John has learnt to play tennis*) is no less anomalous than *John has learnt to speak language* (as opposed to *John has learnt to speak English*).

Some theorists seem to suggest that there is an asymmetry between the rules needed for linguistic production and those needed for comprehension. Bickerton (2009: 77-8) claims that, for purposes of comprehension, you do not need to know that *Go to the refrigerator and get an orange* consists of two coordinate clauses, that *to* introduces a locative phrase, or that *orange* is the direct object of *get*. All you need to know are 'the meanings of four words' (*go, refrigerator, get* and *orange*). He seems to have forgotten that part of the 'meaning' of a word consists in its potential for combining with others. If we take no notice at all of the pattern of combination, the four words might equally mean 'Go and get an orange refrigerator', or 'Go, refrigerator, and get an orange'.

There would be no point in appealing to rules in connexion with language acquisition unless rules were learnable. So learnability has to be somehow incorporated into our concept of a rule. What makes rules learnable? Is it just that – at least in some cases – our conduct can be shown to conform to them? But conformity does not go far enough. We may behave regularly in a certain way for reasons having nothing to do with conforming to a rule. In order to treat a regularity in behaviour as a rule-governed conformity, we have to regard the practice as involving a compulsion or obligation of some kind. What we do has to be the *result* of following the rule.

A further question arises in connexion with rules: 'Are all human activities rule-governed?' The tempting parallel is this. Just as the physical world is law-governed, so human activities are rule-governed. The division of labour sounds initially convincing. Nature makes the laws of physics, while human beings make the rules of society. But this simplistic parallel is an intellectual booby-trap.

If all social activities are rule-governed, language acquisition is not a special case after all, and rules turn out to have a curious status in our lives. They are allegedly ubiquitous and grasped by every learner, even if never articulated, i.e. never overtly recognized as such. Their conscious recognition is (for some reason never explained) quite rare and in any case superfluous. The conspicuous objection to this view is that some rules patently are both articulated and widely discussed: for instance, the rule that forbids theft of other people's property, and many other prohibitions that are recognized in the criminal law of civilized societies. These are legally articulated in great detail – in such detail that it takes years of professional expertise to master them. Rules entail obligations and are enforced by relevant authorities. Their enforcement is complex and often contentious. They are not just simple, consistent *regularities* in observable behaviour. Driving on the left in England would be a regularity, not a rule, if it were not stipulated in the Highway Code.

A visitor to England might not be aware of what is laid down in the Highway Code and conclude that driving on the left was a quaint old English custom, handed down from one generation to the next. What he would be missing is precisely what distinguishes a rule of conduct from a habitual practice. It is knowing the rule – and deciding to observe it – that causes (*pace* Chomsky) the relevant behaviour.

How, then, can anyone be sure that *unarticulated* rules exist? This is the snag in the rule-learning scenario. According to Matthews, the main test for a linguistic rule is that 'when it is broken it is clear how the form would be corrected' (Matthews 2007: 350). The notion of a rule, on this view, is implicitly bound up with recognition of the distinction between 'correct' and 'incorrect'. If this is so, rules and correctness chase one another round in an endless circle, unless there are some forms of correctness that dispense with rules. But we have yet to hear what they are.

According to Chomsky, at a certain stage children 'characteristically overgeneralize', resulting in such forms as *sleeped* for *slept* and *brang* for *brought*. He claims that if all adults were to die from some sudden disease 'the "language would change" and these irregularities would be erased. The child's rule would now be "correct" for the new language' (Chomsky 1986: 227). This is doubly misleading. There is no 'language change' in the situation Chomsky envisages. One language, the adult language, no longer exists. Nor does the child's rule become 'correct'. For there is no longer the former distinction between 'correct' and 'incorrect'.

If the rule-theorists are right, individuals learning their native language presumably cannot make judgments of correctness or incorrectness until they have mastered at least *some* rules. The same seems to apply to other cases of learning, such as learning how to make an omelette or learning how to sew a button on. So the problem is: how does one recognize these first rules – and *ipso facto* that the whole enterprise is rule-governed?

One possibility is that a learner may learn by explicit *instruction*. But this possibility requires a teacher, who *ex hypothesi* knows the rules. That leads straight to a regress. (How does the teacher know them?)

Another possibility is that one learns by one's own mistakes. But this requires that one can recognize mistakes *as* mistakes. Rule-following and making mistakes are head and tail of the same coin. So no progress there.

A third possibility is that one learns by imitating others. But here there is no guarantee that what one has learnt is a rule. Buying a sandwich for lunch because other people often buy sandwiches for lunch is conforming to a widespread social practice, but it does not amount to learning a sandwich rule, unless the rule is 'Buy a sandwich if you want to'. If *Do X if you want to* is a facile formula for setting up rules, it is also a formula for rendering them nugatory.

So whichever way we pursue the idea of what learning a rule involves, there is no light at the end of the tunnel.

According to Fromkin and Rodman:

> Every human being who speaks a language knows the grammar. When linguists wish to describe a language they attempt to describe the grammar of the language which exists in the minds of its speakers. There may of course be some differences between the knowledge that one speaker has and that of another. But there must be shared knowledge because it is this grammar which makes it possible for speakers to talk and understand one another. (Fromkin and Rodman 1974: 9)

Here integrationists will recognize an unacknowledged commitment to the traditional 'language myth' that goes back to Plato and Aristotle (Harris 1981). Postulating that languages are shared sets of rules is an alternative to, or perhaps another version of, what Reddy describes as the 'conduit metaphor' (Reddy 1979). The conduit metaphor, instantiated in dozens of English idioms, assumes that a language is 'like a conduit', through which thoughts are passed from one person to another. Rather than demonstrate that those who understand one another actually speak or write the same language, Fromkin and Rodman simply assume that they must do, *because* they succeed in communicating. But this is plainly circular when communication is tacitly assumed to require mastery of a common language.

Integrationists are committed to no such assumption. B's linguistic practice is never identical with A's. Communication involves an *interpretation* by B of what A has said or written. But B interprets this in his own way, on the basis of his own linguistic experience and of his own contextualization of A's initiative. He has no other technique of interpretation open to him.

18

The use of the word *acquisition* in *language acquisition* is worthy of note. We do not normally speak of *acquiring* trumpet-playing rather than learning to play the trumpet, or of *acquiring* cookery rather than learning to cook. But we speak of acquiring a reputation (e.g. for parsimony) and acquiring likes and dislikes (ice-cream, air travel, etc.). The difference seems to be that what is acquired is a cumulative by-product of other activities. We do not normally have it in our sights and set out to acquire it.

So 'acquiring the rules' verges on self-contradiction, as if we became acquainted with them as a result of doing something *else*. We do not learn to play chess accidentally while in the process of doing something else. Nor is it any more plausible to maintain that we learn to speak our native language accidently while engaged in some unrelated non-linguistic enterprise.

54

Truth and Objectivity

It is sometimes held that truth, unlike objectivity, is an absolute value.

> One theory can be more objective than another. But a theory cannot be truer than another, because truth is an absolute notion: something is either true or it is not. (Gaukroger 2012: 66)

The same author immediately goes on to add, disconcertingly: 'There can of course be degrees of approximation to the truth, but these are not degrees of truth, and so are wholly unlike degrees of objectivity.' Objectivity, he tells us, concerns such matters as freedom from bias and prejudice.

It is difficult to reconcile the philosophical contention that truth is an absolute notion with the commonsense lay view that statements can be *partly* true. If John is suffering from an advanced form of cancer, the statement 'John is ill' is true, but it does not give the whole truth about John's health, although it states nothing false either.

Nor, on the other hand, is it an 'approximation' to the truth. In order to have degrees of approximation to a target or an objective we must have a scale of values applicable in the case in question. Those who realize the seriousness of John's condition may regard 'John is ill' as an understatement. But in illness there is no exact scale to apply. On the other hand, if I say 'It is twelve o'clock' when it is only eleven fifty-five, I am five minutes out. But appreciably nearer the truth than someone who says it is quarter to twelve.

(Nearer, precisely, by ten minutes.) Time and space are the public areas in which we customarily apply scales of measurement. It is not inconceivable that we should have them in health. The National Health Service might allocate everybody a 'health measure' ranging from 1 to 10, according to their GP's assessment. Those patients with severely debilitating illnesses would score 1, while those with 'nothing wrong with them' would score 10.

Aristotle says that 'it is the mark of an educated man to look for precision in each class of things just so far as the nature of the subject permits' (*Nichomachean Ethics* I.3). In the same passage he speaks of things which are 'only for the most part true' and of indicating the truth 'roughly and in outline'. All of this is *prima facie* in conflict with the notion of truth as an absolute.

Paul Horwich (Horwich 1990) presents a 'minimalist' or 'deflationary' theory of truth, intended to divest truth of its mysteries. He holds that 'nothing could be more mundane and less puzzling than the concept of truth'.

> The minimalist view of utterances does not deny that there are such things as propositions, beliefs, truth conditions and possible states of affairs. It maintains only that our conception of truth for utterances does not presuppose them. (Horwich 1990: 12)

Integrationists are deflationists where truth is concerned, but for reasons somewhat different from those advanced by Horwich. Integrationists allow that every individual is free to interpret the words *true* and *truth* (and any other expressions in his or her vocabulary) in his or her own way, and is free to determine the situations to which they are regarded as applicable. Far from truth being absolute, in other words, truth is relative to the viewpoint(s) and interests of those participating in the act of communication. Horwich, on the other hand, believes it to be uncontroversial that *snow is white* is true if and only if snow is white. On his view, one instance of non-white snow would suffice to render *snow is white* false. In other words, he treats *snow is white* as meaning in effect *all snow is white (always and for everybody with normal vision).*

It is commonplace to regard a statement as true if it appears to 'correspond to the facts', where 'the facts' are objectively and independently available. Thus the statement that 'Paris is the capital of France' is held to be true because it is a verifiable political and social fact that the capital of France is indeed Paris.

Austin, however, invites us to consider whether 'the question of truth or falsity is so very objective' (Austin 1962: 141). He asks whether in general 'the good reasons and good evidence for stating and saying (are) so very different from the good reasons and evidence for performative acts like arguing, warning, and judging.'

> Is the constative, then, always true or false? When a constative is confronted with the facts, we in fact appraise it in ways involving the employment of a vast array of terms which overlap with those that we use in the appraisal of performatives. (Austin 1962: 141-2)

Here we detect a double appeal to 'facts'. There are facts with which to 'confront' the constative, and there are facts about the way we appraise it. Austin never tells us how they are related.

From an integrationist perspective, Peter's statement *Snow is white* is acceptable as *Peter's* generalization about snow, provided it holds for all or most snow-judgments Peter is inclined to make. But the *sentence* used (i.e. the English sentence *Snow is white*) is neither true nor false. The integrationist agrees with Austin when he writes:

> It is essential to realize that 'true' and 'false', like 'free' and 'unfree', do not stand for anything simple at all; but only for a general dimension of being a right or proper thing to say as opposed to a wrong thing, in these circumstances, to this audience, for these purposes and with these intentions. (Austin 1962: 144)

23

Furthermore:

In real life, as opposed to the simple situations envisaged in logical theory, one cannot always answer in a simple manner whether it is true or false. (Austin 1962: 142)

Elsewhere Austin holds that

it was only so long as the real nature of mathematical formulae, say, or of geometrical axioms remained unrecognized, and they were thought to record information about the world, that it was reasonable to call them 'true'...: but, once their nature has been recognized, we no longer feel tempted to call them 'true' or to dispute about their truth or falsity. (Austin 1961: 99-100)

Austin may be suspected of a certain amount of casuistry here. For to talk about 'the real nature' of something remaining 'unrecognized' is to say that the truth was overlooked. To regard '2 + 2 = 4' as stating a truth about the world is to say that it captures a generalization about adding two items to another two. And who would deny that it does so?

To some theorists, maintaining that we cannot always say whether something purportedly factual is true may sound as outrageous as saying that a five-pound note is valueless, or at least that is has no fixed value. Indeed the note *is* valueless if the parties to a transaction do not accept payments in sterling. Saussure recognized as much when he proclaimed that *values* (*valeurs*) rest on equivalences between things belonging to different orders, such as work and wages (Saussure 1922: 115). *Value is always exchange-value*. That is the basic theoretical proposition of Saussurean structuralism.

A forged five-pound note is valueless once the forgery is detected, and valueless *because* it was printed by a forger, i.e. by someone not properly authorized. But, equally, work is valueless if no one treats it as useful or desirable. Digging a hole in the ground and filling it in again demands work, but no one will pay for it if it was never required in the first place. It is not 'marketable' or 'valuable' work. Its status is like that of the forged currency note. It lays claim to an exchange-value which it lacks.

According to Horwich (Horwich 1990 :36) a person's understanding of the truth predicate, *is true*, (i.e. his 'knowledge of its meaning') consists in 'his disposition to accept, without evidence, any instantiation of the schema 'The proposition *that p* is true if and only if p' by a declarative sentence of English (including any extension of English)'. Here Horwich ties himself in knots. For even nonsense words would pass his test. (Cf. *The proposition that p is frabulous is true if and only if p is frabulous.* Nor is there any guarantee that *frabulous* may not appear in some future 'extension of English'. An integrationist will contend that it has made its appearance already – namely, in the present paragraph.) Our concept of truth, Horwich concludes, is 'the central component in the state of understanding the word' (i.e. the word *true*). It is 'that component which is independent of language and of the particular word that is employed' (Horwich 1990: 38).

For integrationists, this last proviso is nonsense. There is no component which is 'independent of language and of the particular word that is employed'. According to Horwich, "is true' is a perfectly good English predicate' (Horwich 1990: 38). But he speaks of 'different roles that predicates play in our language'. We should 'beware against assimilating *being true* to such properties as *being turquoise, being a tree,* or *being made of tin*' (Horwich 1990: 39). Horwich distinguishes his view from 'more radical formulations of deflationism – those according to which it is a grammatical illusion to think that *X is true* makes a statement of *any* kind about the proposition X' (Horwich 1990: 39. Italics in the original.)

No integrationist supposes that 'Paris is the capital of France' states the *whole* truth about Paris. But it is (currently) *part of* the whole truth, and is likely to remain so for as long as Paris remains the capital of France. Whether it is an *important* part of the truth brings us back to the question of objectivity. The truth may be construed as the conclusion reached by an ideally objective observer when all the relevant information is known.

Gaukroger attributes to Aenesidemus of Cnossus the view that perception is always relative to (i) the observer, (ii) the conditions of observation and (iii) the state of the object when perceived. There is no way things *really* look, according to Aenesidemus: they look differently to creatures with different organs of vision, and according to the conditions under which they are viewed. Gaukroger seeks a way out of the dilemma.We should resist being forced to choose between saying that the world is just as human sense organs present it and saying that how the world seems to be is completely relative. (Gaukroger 2012: 36). According to Gaukroger 'there is no doubt that there is a grey area between assumptions and prejudices. However, grey areas do not invalidate distinctions.' (Gaukroger 2012: 37). An integrationist would reply that grey areas do not invalidate distinctions as such, but they certainly make their *application* arbitrary, as the Sorites paradox shows.

Rejecting Sorites and declining to choose between trusting the senses and opting for relativism leaves one in a philosophical no-man's-land. There is little virtue in taking up residence in that intellectual location. Nor is there any point in insisting for philosophical purposes on criteria more rigorous than those we adopt in our daily dealings with the world and with others. To believe that philosophy needs more rigorous criteria is to fall into the trap of treating philosophy as a kind of higher-order inquiry which has left everyday language behind.

55

Synchronic / Diachronic

In many university departments of linguistics, teaching and research are still divided between 'synchronic' and 'diachronic', in accordance with the distinction first laid down by Saussure more than a hundred years ago. This distinction is commonly interpreted as depending on whether the passage of time is to be taken into account. To say that the past participle of the French verb *boire* is *bu* counts as a synchronic statement, since it relates two items belonging to the same language at the same time (the present); whereas to say that *boire* comes from Latin *bibere* is a diachronic statement, since it relates items belonging to different languages and different periods.

In the *Cours de linguistique générale*, the distinction is presented in the following terms:

> *Synchronic linguistics* will be concerned with logical and psychological connexions between coexisting items constituting a system, as perceived by the same collective consciousness.
> *Diachronic linguistics* on the other hand will be concerned with connexions between sequences of items not perceived by the same collective consciousness, which replace one another without themselves constituting a system. (Saussure 1922: 140)

The terms which stand out in this programmatic statement are *system* and *collective consciousness*. Both will be discussed further below.

Even professional linguists, who should know better, sometimes misinterpret Saussure as defining synchrony with reference to the present. Urszula Clark, for instance, says that Saussure 'made a distinction between two axes of time in linguistic study: the diachronic axis – the time line of the past, present and future; and the synchronic axis – the time line of the present' (Clark 2007: 142). It is small wonder that the distinction then proves problematic. There is no 'time line of the present'. The present is here one moment and gone the next. As soon as we link a succession of moments or events, we are already thinking diachronically.

Saussure's teaching in Geneva was remarkable for its reliance on vague concepts which Saussure himself had not yet thought through in detail. He himself recognized that 'very few linguists realise that the need to take account of the passage of time gives rise to special problems in linguistics and forces us to choose between two radically different approaches' (Saussure 1922: 114).

Later generations of linguists have always had the greatest difficulty in rationalizing the postulated division between synchrony and diachrony, even when they have not misunderstood Saussure. They tend to cope with it by substituting 'contemporaneous' for 'synchronic' and 'historical' for 'diachronic'. Thus interpreted, there is no longer anything particularly linguistic about the distinction in question. Any study of change will count as 'diachronic', while any study which excludes change becomes 'synchronic'. In fact, Saussure's dichotomy is itself a failed attempt to keep both in play by keeping them rigorously apart.

Where does Saussure go astray? Initially, by treating a subjective difference of *perspective* as an objective difference in what is observed. His epistemology bipartitions what he calls the realm of 'facts', appealing to an absolute distinction between 'facts of evolution' and 'static facts' (i.e. facts pertaining to states). As far as one can see, no facts are allowed to be both.

The consequence of the radical difference between facts of evolution and static facts is that all notions pertinent to the former and all notions pertinent to the latter are mutually irreducible... No synchronic phenomenon has anything in common with any diachronic phenomenon. (Saussure 1922: 129)

If this is to be taken seriously, it would be a mistake (bordering on self-contradiction) to discuss the etymology of any word currently in use. For this involves treating a synchronic form as having a history, indeed as the *product* of its own history. But patently it is no more mistaken to discuss the etymology of a present-day form *in the present* than to talk about the history of a building which is still standing. Nothing obliges us to refrain from talking about a building until it has fallen down or been replaced. It is not just that Saussure has overstated his case, but that his case is incoherent. The confusion is made worse by introducing a third term, *panchronic* (*panchronique*), supposedly to cover relations, if there are any, 'which hold in all cases and forever' (Saussure 1922: 134).

One way of patching up Saussure's position would be to retract the claim that no synchronic phenomenon has anything in common with any diachronic phenomenon. Integrationism, however, resolves the problem, or rather dissolves it, in a different way; namely, by treating all human activities as taking place in the same chronological continuum. This in effect eliminates synchrony. Integrationists call the basis for this theoretical move the 'principle of cotemporality'. (For discussion, see Harris 1998: 61ff.) Once synchrony is eliminated, there is no more need to talk about linguistic 'states'. (See further below.) At the same time, integrationists, in common with many others, are sceptical about invoking a 'collective consciousness'. They rest content with accepting that some attitudes and beliefs are more widespread than others, and see no reason for postulating hypothetical group mentalities to explain this.

Saussure makes it clear that for him synchronic and diachronic studies are not of equal importance. Synchronic studies take precedence. Taking a diachronic point of view, the linguist 'is no longer examining the language (*langue*), but a series of events which modify it' (Saussure 1922: 128).

In the *Cours de linguistique générale* synchrony and diachrony are represented diagrammatically by two orthogonal axes: the 'axis of simultaneities' and the 'axis of successions'. The axis of successions is shown by a continous line running vertically up and down the page, with the axis of successions at right angles to it across the page. According to Saussure the axis of successions contains all the things situated along the other axis, 'together with the changes they undergo' (Saussure 1922: 115). But it is not at all clear how we are supposed to interpret the point where these two axes are shown intersecting.

Introducing this *spatial* image of an intrinsically *temporal* distinction has certain consequences which most Saussurean commentators have been slow to pick up. It is not a gratuitous visual illustration but part of a theoretical manoeuvre which allows Saussure to claim that individual language-users command and exploit a *state* of the language (*état de langue*). And this is Saussure's justification for introducing the opposition synchronic vs. diachronic in the first place. As far as members of the linguistic community are concerned, he tells us, the synchronic point of view is 'the one and only reality'. 'Synchrony has only one perspective, that of the language users; and its whole method consists of collecting evidence from them' (Saussure 1922: 128).

The trouble with this bold claim, an integrationist will say, is that it is not borne out by everyday experience. We may well be ignorant of the history of the forms we use. But, on the other hand, it is illusory to conjure up a single synchronic linguistic state to accommodate all that is left when history is ignored or unknown. We utter sentences one by one, i.e. *in succession*. It takes time. There is no single moment at which any of us can command a panoramic perspective of *all* our current linguistic resources simultaneously.

Nor can a professional linguist carry out this imaginary operation on our behalf. For a professional linguist is required by his profession to be a member of a linguistic community, and as such is limited in exactly the same way as everyone else. Synchronic investigation *takes time*, as does the articulation of every synchronic statement. So the passage of time is as intrinsic to synchrony as it is to diachrony.

The etymology of the term *synchronic* nevertheless prevails in our glossaries of linguistics. According to Matthews, a synchronic description of a language is 'an account of its structure either at present or at some specific moment in the past, considered in abstraction from its history' (Matthews 2007: 396). Campbell and Mixco (2007: 198) tell us that *synchrony* means 'looking at a language at a single point in time'. Neither comments on the difficulty of making sense of the notion of a language existing just at one arbitrarily selected instant. Saussure, however, did recognize the conceptual problem, and revised his original formulation accordingly.

> In practice, a linguistic state occupies not a point in time, but a period of time of varying length, during which the sum total of changes is minimal. It may be ten years, a generation, a century, or even longer. (Saussure 1922: 142)

He could have said more bluntly: 'In practice there is no such thing as a linguistic state...' For he concedes that 'languages are always changing, however minimally' (Saussure 1922: 142). Instead, however, he introduces the pseudo-scientific term *idiosynchronique*, stipulating that it shall be understood as referring not to everything simultaneous, but 'only the set of facts corresponding to any particular language' (Saussure 1922: 128). Immediately, the horizontal 'axis of simultaneities' is divested of its purely temporal significance and becomes an abstraction defined solely by contrast with its orthogonal counterpart (the vertical line). There is no matching term *idiodiachronique*, since according to Saussure diachronic linguistics deals with items which do not necessarily belong to a single language (Saussure 1922: 129). Far from it. In fact, says Saussure,

> In the diachronic perspective one is dealing with phenomena which have no connexion with linguistic systems, even though the systems are affected by them. (Saussure 1922: 122)

So the basic, indispensable opposition turns out to be not 'synchronic vs. diachronic' after all, but 'single language' vs. 'no single language'. This opposition is neither synchronic nor diachronic. It is not even panchronic. It has nothing to do with time or the passage of time.

Saussure makes no attempt to spell out what range of individual diversity is acceptable within the confines of a 'single language'. All he observes is that 'languages have no natural boundaries' (Saussure 1922: 278), which does not make the notion of a 'single language' any easier to pin down. It is impossible to imagine, he tells us, 'in any shape or form a precise linguistic boundary dividing an area covered throughout by evenly differentiated dialects' (Saussure 1922: 279). That rules out any prospect of giving 'single language' an exact geographical interpretation.

But nor does it lend itself to an exact temporal interpretation. The trouble with 'the present' is that it is constantly receding into 'the past'. But we enlarge or restrict its scope at will, according to our immediate concerns. Yesterday is already in the past, but we can refer to it as being in 'the present week', 'the present month' or 'the present century'. These expressions relate what has already gone by to present moment. One might ask: how long does it take a 'single language' to establish itself in the present? But it is difficult to know where to look for an answer. The very question 'how long does it take?' introduces a diachronic perspective.

The synchronic/diachronic problem is not intrinsically tied to Saussurean structuralism. It arises also for behaviourists who construe speech habits in terms of observable stimuli and responses. The austere logic of this approach gives even Bloomfield pause. At one point he concedes: 'The practical situations which make up the meaning of a speech-form are not strictly definable: one could say that every utterance of a speech-form involves a minute semantic innovation' (Bloomfield 1935: 407). Thus it seems we deceive ourselves if we think we can repeat exactly what we said a minute ago. *Everything* we say ushers in a new, if fleeting, *état de langue*. Bloomfield's 1923 review of the *Cours de linguistique générale* is one of the most interesting documents in 20th-century linguistics. It is not that Bloomfield rejects or questions Saussure's holistic conception of *la langue*: he does not even notice it. Saussure's famous statement that 'a language (*langue*) is a system of which all the parts can and must be considered as synchronically interdependent' is allowed to pass without comment. There is no more striking illustration of how behaviourism serves its adherents as a linguistic blindfold.

But the dilemma is even more acute for the Saussurean structuralist, i.e. the dilemma of reconciling the notion of synchrony with a holistic conception of the 'state' of the language. It is implausible to treat the lexicon as if it were a finite list. But Saussure is not reluctant to declare that each language constitutes a closed system (Saussure 1922: 139), as he must do if every unit is defined contrastively with the rest. We cannot bring 'the rest' into the equation if the rest is unknown.

Lay experience suggests, in any case, that our vocabulary is open-ended. If we read widely, we learn new words every day, as well as new uses of old words. The repertoire of sentences available to us increases accordingly. Even one new word adds many new potential sentences. Thus, apparently, we go through an endless succession of *états de langue*, perhaps two or more in a single day. Each new word or new use, according to Saussure, automatically brings about a minor readjustment in relations with the expressions

33

available previously. We cannot add to – or subtract from – an existing lexical stock without restructuring the whole, since the units are not defined independently, but *contrastively* with one another. Saussure's conclusion is that 'no linguistic item can be based, ultimately, upon anything other than its non-coincidence with the rest' (Saussure 1922: 163). We cannot tell what language we shall be speaking tomorrow, because tomorrow 'the rest' may be different.

If we follow Saussure's thinking thus far, the question then arises of whether our supposedly 'new' coinages were not already in the lexicon, waiting to be used. Saussure seems to have envisaged something of the kind.

> When a new word such as *indécorable* ('undecoratable') crops up in speech... it presupposes an already existing type, and the type in question would not exist were it not for our recollection of a sufficient number of similar words already in the language, e.g. *impardonnable* ('unpardonable'), *intolérable* ('intolerable'), *infatigable* ('indefatigable'), etc. (Saussure 1920: 173)

There is a certain now-you-see-it-now-you-don't about this explanation. For if the type 'IN + root + ABLE' already exists in French linguistic consciousness, the eventual public occurrence of the form *indécorable* brings about no change in the structure of that part of the vocabulary.

> Any creation has to be preceded by an unconscious comparison of materials deposited in the store held by the language (*langue*), where the sponsoring forms are arranged by syntagmatic and associative relations.
> So one whole part of the phenomenon has already been completed before the new form becomes visible. The continual activity of language (*langage*) in analysing the units already provided contains in itself not only all possibilities of speaking in conformity with

usage, but also all possibilities of analogical formation.
(Saussure 1922: 227)

This threatens the distinction between synchrony and diachrony even more radically. For it now sounds as if each language (*langue*), by virtue of its present structure, has its future, or perhaps several possible futures, ready in advance.
The passage of time extends forward into the unknown as well as backwards into the past.

The related problem which Saussure fails to address is how to explain the origin of these 'types' which already exist. He simply takes their existence for granted. Chalker and Weiner tackle the issue head on and suggest that neologisms have the following eight sources: abbreviation, back-formation, blending, borrowing, clipping, compounding, conversion (e.g. verb from noun), and derivation. They add that the term *neologism* is sometimes extended to include old words given new meanings (Chalker and Weiner 1994: 225).

If Chalker and Weiner's account is on the right lines, it follows that most so-called 'neologisms' are not strictly new. They are formed from existing lexical sources by processes widely implemented already in the linguistic community. So the term *neologism* fails to capture the fact that at some point types must have arisen which had *no* precedents or models in existing usage. These are what we might call 'absolute neologisms'.

When, for example, did our ancestors first use a suffix to indicate plurality? Or when did they first join together sequentially the components of a simple sentence and thus form the archetypal Subject-Predicate construction? To argue that there was no 'first time' in these cases is to suppose that grammars come fully formed into human consciousness, and that compositionality is there from the beginning.

The underlying problem in all of this is that the distinction between synchrony and diachrony collapses unless we are prepared to treat the totality of a community's linguistic resources at any one time as a single, internally consistent system (Saussure's *état*). But all 'systems' are intellectual constructs or the physical realizations of such constructs (a transport system, a currency system, an educational system, etc.). What we say or write is no exception. We envisage our linguistic resources as a system by focussing on the regularities and ignoring any irregularities or treating them as 'exceptions'.

Bloomfield puts it differently and avoids invoking systems:

> Since we have no way of defining most meanings and of demonstrating their constancy, we have to take the specific and stable character of language as a presupposition of linguistic study, just as we presuppose it in our everyday dealings with people. (Bloomfield 1935: 144)

But whether we talk of 'states' or 'presuppositions of constancy' makes little difference. If we opt for states, the question is: a state *of what* exactly? It is not a state of mind in the usually accepted sense of that expression, for states of mind are states of individual minds: they are temporary states and can change unpredictably. A state of the brain? But brains too belong to individuals, and states of the brain are not readily observable. Likewise if we opt for 'constancy', we incur an obligation to explain constancy *in what?*

No individual is ever in a position to identify on the basis of his or her own experience exactly what belongs to English usage at any given point in time and what does not. Individuals have no personal monopoly on English usage. But it sounds superficially more plausible to suppose that, acting in concert, *all* English speakers and writers might be able to reach linguistic agreement about how in practice they speak and write. This is the gap that Saussure attempts to plug by appealing to the existence of a 'collective consciousness'. It is an appeal which removes linguistics from empirical investigation altogether and relegates it to cloud-cuckoo-land. The seemingly simplistic distinction between synchrony and diachrony brings us straight away up against the limits of our understanding of language. Here if anywhere we begin to encounter what Colin McGinn calls problems that 'exceed our cognitive competence' (McGinn 2004: 110).

56

On Lexicography

The dictionary is a perplexing work of reference in many ways. For a start, it assumes that you already know the spelling of the word you want to 'look up', or at least have a rough idea of how it is spelt. That is why dictionary entries are arranged in alphabetical order. There is no compelling *linguistic* reason for this arrangement. It is purely a matter of practical convenience, on a par with the listing of names in a telephone directory or the numbering of houses in the same street. But whereas house numbers are based on the physical locations of houses, there is no corresponding 'real world' feature which explains the sequential place of a headword in a dictionary. Nor is A, B, C, D, E... like 1, 2, 3, 4, 5... In the numerical sequence, each unit bears a fixed arithmetic relation to the units on either side. Nothing of the kind obtains in the sequence of letters. Alphabetical order is arbitrary, although in a quite different sense from Saussure's *arbitraire* (Saussure 1922: 100).

But that is not all. As a dictionary user you are expected to understand that it is of no *linguistic* significance whether a particular entry appears on page 29 or on page 30. Page numbering is not peculiar to dictionaries and relates to the physical properties of the dictionary as a book. How much the printer can put on each page depends on the type face employed and the page size, not on the fact that it appears in a dictionary.

We are dealing here with the integration of two sets of assumptions: the user's and the lexicographer's. If there is a serious mismatch between those assumptions, the dictionary becomes useless. The assumptions discussed so far relate to the dictionary as a physical artifact.

However, there are also properties of a dictionary which reflect its linguistic function, and these take pride of place in the theory of lexicography. When you look up a word in a dictionary you expect to be authoritatively informed of its orthography and its meaning. Some dictionaries also attempt to tell you how it is pronounced. But consulting a dictionary is so familiar that users rarely reflect on exactly how they have to interpret the dictionary entry if it is to fulfil these various functions.

The *linguistic* requirements are more complex than is obvious at first sight. There are at least four Dictionary headwords have to be simultaneously
(i) Peircean types *and* tokens,
(ii) 'object language' units *and* 'metalanguage' units,
(iii) examples of *both* 'use' *and* 'mention',
(iv) elements of a language system (*langue*) *as well as* parts of a particular text (the dictionary itself being that text).

The requirement of simultaneity means that, as found in dictionaries, headwords bridge (or challenge) at least four distinctions commonly accepted in modern linguistics. It is not up to us to decide how to consider them. *Quite the opposite.* We have no choice in the matter. This will become evident if each requirement is considered in turn.

(i) *Types and tokens.* The distinction between types and tokens, originally proposed by C.S. Peirce, involves recognizing five word-tokens in the sentence *I said I would come,* but only four word-types, since the first person pronoun *I* occurs twice. When we 'look up' a word we are looking for a type, but we find it represented by a token of that type. The type/token distinction is explicitly formulated with writing in mind, being based on two ways of counting how many words there are in a printed text – the printer's calculation and the lexicographer's. Every word-token takes up space in the text, which the printer must allow for; whereas the lexicographer does not include a separate entry for each. Every headword counts as one token for the printer, just like any other word in the entry. But it also identifies the word-type which the lexicographer is attempting to explicate. There is no divorcing these two functions: they are intrinsic to the reflexivity of language, on which the dictionary is based. A parallel case can be found in a botanical catalogue which gives separate photographs of all the flowers for sale. In the catalogue a picture of a flower is both a token of one actual flower and at the same time a type of the species on offer. If we place an order we do not expect to buy the flower shown in the photograph, but a flower or flowers of the same species.

(ii) *Object language and metalanguage.* According to Matthews, a metalanguage is:

> a language used to make statements about a language. The language about which they are made is correspondingly the object language... Thus a Spanish grammar of English uses Spanish, or a variety of Spanish, as a metalanguage for the description of English: in an English grammar written in English, the same language is both metalanguage and object language. (Matthews 2007: 243)

The terms are profoundly misleading. Metalanguage and object language are not languages at all, but ways of using words. The error is on a par with calling eggs omelettes. Metalinguistic statements are the *raison d'être* of a dictionary. What might be called the 'metalinguistic paradox' is that no one would buy a dictionary which gave 'cat' as the meaning of *cat*, although that is arguably the most exact and concise definition it is possible to give. If a headword could be only one *or* the other, it would have to be either part of the metalanguage or part of the object language, but not both. This would make nonsense of the lexicographer's entry.

(iii) *Use and mention.* According to Matthews, mention is 'the use of a word etc. to refer to itself' (Matthews 2007: 242). He omits to specify whether the reference is to itself as a token, or to itself as a type. The illustration provided is *The cat is in the garden* as an example of *using* the word *cat*; and *What is the definition of 'cat'?* as an example of *mentioning* the word. Mention is commonly marked in writing by enclosing the item mentioned in inverted commas. There is no corresponding oral device in speech. In practice the distinction between use and mention is often blurred, as when writers italicize their first use of a technical term or put it in bold type or inverted commas. This practice might be called 'pseudo-mention', of which this sentence provides an example. The pseudo-mentioned form does not hover somewhere in between use and mention, or alternate between the two, like the philosopher's famous duck-rabbit, but incorporates both.

(iv) *System and text.* For those who prefer Saussurean terminology, this distinction can be expressed as *langue* vs. *parole* (extending Saussure's terms to cover writing and well as speech). The dictionary headword belongs to both system and text. It identifies a lexical unit in the language system being described, while at the same time being part of the description offered by the lexicographer. If it could be only one *or* the other (exclusive disjunction), the headword would either fail to identify the word described or fail to be part of the lexicographer's text. Both are equally absurd. If the entry were present but failed to identify the lexical item we were looking for, we should be on a wild goose chase. If it were not part of the lexicographer's text, we should not be able to look it up anyway. The only remedy for either defect is to buy a better dictionary.

If the above remarks (i) – (iv) are sound, the epistemology of the dictionary manifests at least four aspects of what is often called the reflexivity of language. J.R. Firth was fond of describing linguistics as language 'turned back upon itself' (Firth 1957). It is difficult to know how a human faculty can be 'turned back upon itself', unless that means no more than, for example, looking at one's eyes in a mirror and calling that a case of vision turned back upon itself. But what Firth had in mind is more likely to have been the potential for self-reference, of which the dictionary offers endless examples. Every entry for a word W provides a self-reference to W, i.e. shows W as the headword.

Properties of the word *cat* are not properties of cats. Nor the other way round. But, as students frequently point out, dictionaries usually include both, as if facts about cats all counted as part of the meaning of *cat*. Linguists, on the other hand, distinguish what is rather pompously called 'encyclopaedic knowledge' as 'knowledge of the world'. Knowledge of the world is set apart from knowledge of the language system (Matthews 2007: 122). The implication of the term *encyclopaedic* is that such knowledge properly belongs in an encyclopaedia (which excuses the lexicographer from dealing with it). According to Matthews, encyclopaedic knowledge about cats would include knowing that the young of cats are born blind, that the period of gestation in the domestic cat is about 65 days, and so on.

A case can be made for doubting whether any such distinction can be drawn once and for all. If, for example, it turned out that cats were the only animals currently known who had a gestation period of about 65 days *and* gave birth to blind offspring one might conclude that these two features jointly provided necessary and sufficient conditions for calling a creature a *cat*. But subsequent work in biology could well reveal many more facts unique to cats, as well as a wider distribution of the two features previously thought to be exclusively characteristic of cats.

Lexicography is an open-ended inquiry, as are the various sciences that supply it with material. Knowledge does not come to a pre-ordained stop in any civilization. That is why no dictionary is definitive and no definition either.

57

Thoughts Immaculate

Throughout the Western tradition, thinking has often been construed as a silent form of inner monologue. This goes all the way back to Socrates' definition of thinking as 'talk which the soul has with itself' (*Theaetetus* 189e). It inevitably reminds the modern reader of J.B. Watson's behaviourist thesis that thinking is 'nothing but talking to ourselves' (Watson 1924: 238). But Socrates was no behaviourist, and Watson was no Socrates.

If the soul engages in talk with itself, does it have a language in which to formulate questions and answers? Socrates may have thought that the soul talks to itself in Greek. But Watson insisted that the whole body does our thinking: *'we could still think in some sort of way even if we had no words'* (Watson 1924: 268. Italics in the original.) Does this mean that that thinking, even when eventually expressed in words, is a prior, autonomous activity, i.e. in itself independent of words?

Thoughts, as Stephen Mumford points out 'seem to require no spatial attributes' (Mumford 2012: 69). This is what allows us to think of them as bodiless entities, somehow present in the mind, but taking up no space there, and hence potentially infinite in number. We cannot sit down and think all possible thoughts. We should die long before the task was accomplished. The utility of thoughts resides in our uncanny ability to produce the thought needed at the time we need it.

According to Donald Davidson, 'neither language nor thinking can be fully explained in terms of the other, and neither has conceptual priority' (Davidson 1975: 8). Davidson does not hold that in order to interpret each other's utterances, two speakers have to have a common language. On this point integrationists will agree with him. The notion of a common language belongs to the language myth of the Western tradition. It is chiefly based on extrapolation from language names. Thus if Smith speaks English and Jones speaks English they are often assumed to speak 'the same language'. This is fallacious, an integrationist will say, for it fails to allow for Smith's English being different from Jones's. It may differ in pronunciation, grammar and vocabulary. It may even differ to such an extent that Smith and Jones cannot understand each other, while still retaining enough linguistic features to make it describable as 'English', rather than 'French' or 'Swahili'.

Davidson sets great store by what he calls the 'autonomy of meaning'. Autonomy of meaning, he claims, is 'essential to language'. What he means by that is by no means clear. He also holds that 'only a creature that can interpret speech can have the concept of a thought'. This is no clearer. For there is no unified ability that consists in 'interpreting speech'. What we interpret are particular *speech acts*. And being able to interpret some speech acts is no guarantee of being able to interpret others, let alone all.

There are theorists who postulate a ubiquitous, universal 'language of thought' (often called 'Mentalese'). The existence of Mentalese is something of an enigma. No one has ever produced an example of it. Nor is it available to introspection. What, then, are its credentials? They rest on an argument from analogy, as J.A. Fodor, its principal proponent, concedes in his controversial book *The Language of Thought*:

> There is an analogy between learning a second language
> on the basis of a first and learning a first language on
> the basis of an innate endowment. (Fodor 1976: 59)

Where the analogy breaks down, however, is in the gratuitous assumption that the 'innate endowment' itself takes the form of a language. This what Fodor proposes.

Learning a language (including of course a first language) involves learning what the predicates of the language mean. Learning what the predicates of a language mean involves learning a determination of the extension of these predicates. Learning a determination of the extension of the predicates involves learning that they fall under certain rules (i.e., truth rules). But one cannot learn that *P* falls under *R* unless one has a language in which *P* and *R* can be represented. So one cannot learn a language unless one has a language. (Fodor 1976: 64)

This must rank among the worst arguments ever published in the field of philosophy of language. It leads straight to a regress. For if we cannot learn English unless we already have a 'language of thought', that proviso requires us to have a *further* language in which to formulate the language of thought itself. And so on endlessly. The number of languages required to learn English proliferates *ad infinitum*.

This is not the only problem, however. Another is that Fodor somehow knows in advance that all languages have such things as 'predicates', that predicates have 'representations' and 'extensions', and that extensions have 'determinations' and 'truth rules'. This conceptual baggage that he attaches to the notion of a language includes all the assumptions he will call upon to explain how a language is learnt. In this way he has already made the explanatory task trivial. The possibility he seems to have overlooked is that the 'language of thought' might be a non-verbal system of some kind, i.e. a system whose elements and relations have none of the basic features we associate with English or any other language.

A quite different approach is sketched in the following paragraph from Lycan's *Philosophy of Language*.

People all over the world may believe that Asian markets are collapsing, doubt that Asian markets are collapsing, hope or fear that Asian markets are collapsing.

Do all these people speak or read English? According to Lycan, it does not matter because:

> They could have thought it in any language; it would still be true that they believed, doubted or whatever that Asian markets are collapsing. (Lycan 2008: 70)

Here there is no appeal to a 'language of thought'. Lycan's contention falls under what is sometimes called the 'principle of effability' (Mautner 1997: 160). There is nothing special about the thought of Asian markets collapsing. Lycan's version of effability maintains, in effect, that *any* thought expressable in English can be expressed in *all* languages. (NB. It does not deny that there could be thoughts which elude linguistic expression altogether. But we are not told whether there are such thoughts.)

The obvious empirical objection to Lycan's claim is that there may be – and almost certainly are – languages which have no expressions for 'Asia' or for 'market', let alone for the metaphor of markets 'collapsing'. Defenders of Lycan might argue that what actually happens when Asian markets collapse can be rephrased in terms more amenable to translation, avoiding the words *Asian*, *market* and *collapse*. However, this is not actually the issue. The effability thesis is, precisely, that the particular thought about Asian markets can be thought and expressed in all languages (i.e. languages like French, German and Swahili), *not* that it can somehow be reformulated in different words without loss of content. The question remains: what does thinking this thought consist in?

Is the thought itself independent of *any* form of linguistic expression? Some evidently think so. It is generally agreed that painters, musicians and other artists all think about their art, but not necessarily in words. A scene to be painted may be planned visually in the mind, or a melody composed first in the imagination. But it is

48

difficult to see how a thought such as 'Asian markets are collapsing' could be entertained in some non-verbal form. The claim cannot be understood in the first place unless we treat the words 'Asian markets are collapsing' as expressing it. One cannot even suggest a substitute form of words without first understanding these.

So *prima facie* there is some doubt about whether anyone can *think* that 'Asian markets are collapsing' without somehow engaging with the relevant verbal expression. The thought seems to lose its identity once divorced from the words used to articulate it. Even less can the thought in question be communicated to someone else without having a verbal formulation available. It does not lend itself to gesture or pictorial expression.

Some have argued that it is a mistake to suppose that

a sentence having the meaning that Socrates is a man has to look like the sentence "Socrates is a man" ... So why couldn't it exist as a neuronal firing pattern in the brain? (Feser 2006: 150)

The crucial objection to this is that there is no such thing as a *sentence* meaning that Socrates is a man. From an integrationist perspective, sentences as such do not have meanings. Meanings attach to sayings (utterances) or writings (inscriptions), i.e. to concrete physical events in discourse. What these events mean is determined not by anything registered in advance in dictionaries and grammar books, but by the circumstances and the purposes of the discourse in question at the time and place when it occurs. Sentences, on the other hand, are timeless metalinguistic abstractions. They have no authors. They are addressed to no one. They have no place in first-order discourse.

Speaking and writing are *activities*, as are listening and reading. Doubtless these activities involve what Feser calls 'neuronal firing patterns in the brain'. But so too does everything that engages our senses of sight, hearing, touch, etc. Thinking is also an activity, whether it is conducted verbally or non-verbally.

Thinking too doubtless involves neuronal firing patterns in the brain. But we know nothing about them or their relations with *what* we are thinking.

The Mentalese hypothesis has been rejected on the following ground. If we take mental states to be states of 'a computer program whose causal efficacy derives entirely from their implementation in electrochemical processes in the brain' (Feser 2006: 150-1), an awkward consequence follows. This is that the meanings of the symbols are

> completely irrelevant to their causal efficacy, for they would have the same causal properties whatever meanings they had, or even if they had no meanings. (Feser 2006: 151)

Nothing, in short, guarantees that any neuronal firing pattern corresponds to what we regard as a verbal meaning.

Where does all that leave us? It should leave us convinced that the computational analogy is another red herring where language is concerned. Computers and calculators are very useful instruments. But they do not *understand* what they do, any more than clocks and watches, fire alarms, thermometers or pencil sharpeners. That is not their job.

Such devices as those just mentioned are designed to carry out or facilitate the execution of certain physical operations. A computer has been described as 'any device capable of carrying out a sequence of operations in a defined manner' (Blackburn 1996: 71). It could, for instance, simply turn a switch on and off at intervals, or raise a lever up and down. The operations in question become meaningful only when integrated into wider programmes of human activity.

It is doubtless true that the watchmaker intended your watch to be used as a chronometer, and designed it accordingly. Nevertheless, however accurately your watch *keeps* time, it cannot *tell* the time. Only you can tell the time (if you know how to read the dial and are sure which time zone you are in). Merely describing the positions of the hour hand and the minute hand is not telling the time, any more than being able to describe the shape of the letter N is being able to pronounce it.

Nor, by the same reasoning, can your pocket calculator count. But your calculator was designed by someone who *could* count and devised a way of embodying that ability in a set of mechanical operations to save you the trouble. If your calculator is in working order, it never makes mistakes, whereas you make mistakes all too easily.

It would be wrong to think that the way your calculator operates is restricted to the operations of arithmetic. It could just as easily be designed to give 5 as the total of 2 + 2, or 3 as the square root of 49. That would be perverse of the designer, but not beyond beyond his capabilities. It could also be designed to produce random sequences of letters or numerals. In short, there is no intrinsic connexion between the device itself and the utility of its products. The very same methods by which the calculator operates could be deployed to generate nonsense.

As Robert Martin observes, 'providing an account of the source of our knowledge of arithmetic, and of the kind of facts arithmetical truths report, has always provided a challenge for philosophers' (Martin 2010: 54). Nevertheless, a human consensus about the basic arithmetical operations is what makes calculators viable (and marketable), not vice versa. Their convenience and popularity should not blind anyone to the fact that human beings were thinking about problems in arithmetic long before calculators were invented. Whoever invented the abacus invented a device to save the mental effort of carrying figures 'in your head'.

It seems indisputable that thinking about a problem in arithmetic requires a grasp of the language of arithmetic, including signs for the numerals (1, 2, 3, 4, 5, etc.) and for the various arithmetical operations (+, −, x, etc.). Does it demand these particular signs? This question brings us to the Saussurean doctrine of arbitrariness. If the signs of arithmetic are arbitrary in the Saussurean sense, any other set of signs would do just as well, provided they allowed the same calculations.

The doctrine of arbitrariness, however, does not command universal assent. Benveniste argues that there is 'a contradiction between the way in which Saussure defined the linguistic sign and the fundamental nature he attributed to it' (Benveniste 1939). The contradiction, according to Benveniste, resides in the fact that Saussure smuggled in an appeal to external reality, where he appeared to be treating languages as independent systems of forms. To say that the linguistic sign is arbitrary because the same animal is called *boeuf* on one side of the frontier and *Ochs* on the other, says Benveniste, is like saying that mourning is arbitrary because in Europe it is symbolized by black, but in China by white.

In another essay ('Catégories de pensée et catégories de langue'), Benveniste affirms his view that however abstract or specialized the operations of thought may be, 'they receive expression in language. We can say everything, and we can say it as we wish' (Benveniste 1955: 55) 'Strictly speaking, thought is not matter to which language lends form, since at no time could this "container" be imagined as empty of its contents, nor the "contents" as independent of their "container" (Benveniste 1955: 56).

In the case of the signs of arithmetic, what 'reality' corresponds to the animal in the *boeuf/Ochs* example? There is no parallel in the case of *cinq* and *fünf*, for numbers are themselves intellectual abstractions. They can hardly be invoked to prove their own 'reality'. What justifies equating numerals across different languages is their identical use in counting and other calculations. The arithmetic we learn at school is a system of calculation which incorporates its own language. That is why we learn the same arithmetic irrespective of the native language that we happen to speak. Words such as 'one', 'two', 'three', etc. are simply English translations of symbols ('1', '2', '3', etc.) which belong to the language of arithmetic.

Benveniste, for his part, declares that the connexion between signifier and signified is not arbitrary but necessary. By 'necessary' he apparently means that the link between them is so intimate that it is impossible to think of one without automatically thinking of the other. If so, it should be quite impossible to *forget* what a word means. But everyday experience suggests that it is all too easy.

* * *

The ultimate problem with thoughts is the problem of counting them: it is the only problem that throws light on what thoughts are. Whether *Brutus killed Caesar* and *Caesar was killed by Brutus* are (a) two different thoughts or (b) one and the same thought is a question no one can answer. To be sure, we can choose between (a) and (b) *for certain purposes*, but these purposes do not include elucidating what a thought is in itself.

Opting for (a) involves giving priority to the verbal forms in which these thoughts are expressed in English. But how about a language which has no passive construction? Does the status of thoughts depend on the language in which they are expressed? Should we say that (a) is right only for languages like English, and (b) right otherwise? But then we appear to be answering a different question: a question not about thoughts themselves but about their verbal expression.

In short we cannot disengage these two options. It is instructive to compare this with a different conundrum. Is the glass half empty? Or is it half full? Whatever system of fluid measurement we employ, the answer is 'Both'. But we cannot go for this answer in the case of (a) and (b). For that commits us straight away to self-contradiction.

The metaphysical conclusion to which this leads is rarely acknowledged by philosophers. Appearances to the contrary, thoughts are *intrinsically non-denumerable*. This marks at the same time one of the boundaries of human thinking in general and one of the boundaries of mathematics in particular.

58

What-Is-It-Like?

Thomas Nagel's controversial paper 'What is it like to be a bat?' (Nagel 1974) has the rare distinction of being a philosophical discussion devoted to a question that its author admits is nonsensical. The form of the question invites a comparison (between being a bat and something else, e.g. a human being). But, says Nagel, 'the analogical form of the English expression "what is it *like*" is misleading. It does not mean "what (in our experience) it *resembles*," but rather "how it is for the subject himself". 'I want to know what it is like for a *bat* to be a bat.' (Italics in the original.)

Nagel's question thus explicated is even sillier than one might have thought. For what it is like *for a bat* to be a bat is, unsurprisingly, that it is just like being a bat. It is difficult to see how it could be anything else. That tautology tells us nothing at all about bats or ourselves. Nor does it tell us whether one bat understands what it is like to be another bat. Does being a bat mean having a bat's point of view on the world? Are bats creatures capable of having a point of view?

The choice of the *what is it like?* formula encourages Nagel's readers to assume that the underlying issue (the author's protests notwithstanding) is how far *we* can imagine what a bat's life is like, i.e. within the limits of our non-bat-like imagination. What fascinates Nagel (although he is curiously reluctant to come clean about it) is how far the human imagination is limited by the physical properties of the human form. To what extent can we extrapolate from our own physical being to put ourselves in the make-believe position of quite different creatures? Can we imagine spending a great deal of time hanging up-side-down, or finding our way about by echo-location? Or do we deceive ourselves into thinking that we can imagine it?

According to John Dupré, 'much of this 'what it is like' talk' is a perfect illustration of the 'fallacy of reification'.

> From the possibility, sometimes, of saying what it is like to have particular experiences, we conclude that there is something this is like, and we then try to characterize this entity. (Dupré 2009: 235)

Bennett and Hacker argue that

> it is misconceived to suppose that one can circumscribe, let alone define, *conscious experience* in terms of there being something which it is like for a subject to have it. It does not matter whether 'conscious experience' is understood as 'experience had while conscious' or as 'experience of which one is conscious'. The very expression 'There is something it is like for a person to have it' is malconstructed. (Bennett and Hacker 2003: 277-8. Italics in the original.)

Here the neologism *malconstructed* is not without interest. It is an attempt to avoid the word *ungrammatical*. The charge of ungrammaticality will not stick; but Bennett and Hacker still want to put the blame somehow on the linguistic formulation. Arguably, this is the wrong place to put it. The fault lies rather, as Dupré sees, in the reification of 'what it is like'.

Nagel says that 'our own experience provides the basic material for our imagination, whose range is therefore limited' (Nagel 1974: 394). But he has missed the more fundamental question of whether, even within that range, a mere exercise of the imagination can itself transform our point of view. As an intelligent creature who spends most of its time upright, you understand *what it is* to hang upside-down. You can even try hanging upside-down yourself. That is not the issue. The issue is whether that

56

understanding enables you to adopt the perspective of an unintelligent creature who, quite unlike you, perforce spends a great deal of time hanging upside-down.

The most plausible answer is 'No', because merely hanging habitually upside-down does not enable a creature to appreciate how its life compares with that of any of the many species whose posture is habitually upright.

We can simulate blindness temporarily by the simple expedient of closing our eyes. But human beings with normal vision cannot imagine what it is like to be blind from birth. Nor can individuals blind from birth imagine what it is like to have the gift of sight. Our imaginations, as Nagel says, are at the mercy of our senses. What we can construct in our imaginations depends on our experience of what is usually the case *for us*. We can imagine a flying horse because we are already familiar with horses and with birds. But it is doubtful whether we can imagine *being* a flying horse.

What we call 'imagination' is nothing more than the capacity for hypothesizing that reality is other than what we assume it to be. But the hypothesis does not 'take us in'. We are conscious that it is only imagination, however convincing it seems.

Imaginings have something in common with illusions. According to Robert Martin, when you are seeing an illusion, 'you're aware of something's having a characteristic which the real physical object out there, which you're supposedly perceiving, does not have' (Martin 2010: 118). He adds: 'But as far as your experience goes, there's no difference between how it seems when you're seeing an illusion and when you're perceiving in the ordinary way – in normal, non-illusory situations.'

Martin's analysis is a muddle. A straight stick looks bent when partly immersed in water. But according to Martin there is no way to distinguish from your visual experience whether it is bent or not. Perhaps this is so if you have never seen a stick protruding from a glass of water before. But once you have seen this a few times, and convinced yourself that immersion in water does not bend the stick, you learn to take account of whether the object is seen through air or through water, just as you learn to take account of how far away a building is. You are no longer deceived by appearances, i.e. by the misleading characteristics of the retinal image. If you were, you would see the world the wrong way up, and believe that a ship gets smaller as it sails into the distance.

There is clearly a difference between an illusion that might be veridical and one that could not be. There might be an illusory pint of milk on your doorstep, but there could not be a pink elephant. On 'perceiving' the latter, you immediately realize that something is amiss.

What underlies Martin's muddle is a naive view of perception. But he is not the only theorist to propound one. According to Blackburn, we believe that perception

> gives us knowledge of the world around us. We are
> conscious of that world by being aware of 'sensible
> qualities': colours, sounds, tastes, smells, felt warmth
> and the shapes and positions of objects in the
> environment' (Blackburn 1996: 280)

If that were the case without qualification, our knowledge of the world would be a complex of deceptions. Perceptions are always *interpretations*: they are rarely if ever unprocessed reports from the senses. The interpretations are accommodated and adjusted to background assumptions that we have learned to take for granted as part of our daily experience. There is a good Darwinian reason for this. There would be no advantage to the species in perpetuating over and over again the mistakes about the world that would otherwise accrue. Sticks do not bend when immersed in water any more than ships get smaller when sailing off towards the horizon.

Another version of the *what-is-it-like?* argument comes from Daniel Dennett:

58

It is beyond serious dispute... that you and I each have a mind. How do I know you have a mind? Because anybody who can understand my words is automatically addressed by my pronoun "you", and only things with minds can understand... That's how I know that you, gentle reader/listener have a mind. So do I. Take my word for it. (Dennett 1996: 8)

This is Dennett's account of 'what it is like' to have a mind. Few will be inclined to take his word for it. He is mistaken to suppose that it is 'beyond serious dispute' that we have minds. Donald Davidson, for one, maintains that 'there are no such things as minds' (Davidson 1994: 231). If Davidson is right, the enterprise of demonstrating 'what it is like' to have a mind is doomed in advance to failure. Dennett's argument is not very convincing anyway, for he equates what-it-is-like to have a mind with being able to understand Dennett's statements. If we take this at face value, we are led to conclude that Dennett's grasp of English grammar is lamentably weak. For it is patently *not* the case that anyone who can understand Dennett's words is 'automatically addressed' by his pronoun *you*.

There are two possibilities to consider here. Either (a) Dennett understands his own words, or (b) he does not. Possibilities (a) and (b) are mutually exclusive. If we are charitable and assume (a), that does not make Dennett an addressee, unless he is talking to himself. If we are less charitable and assume (b), we need no longer concern ourselves with what he says, because he is talking nonsense. Whichever option we take, Dennett has offered us no criteria for *judging* whether we understand him or not. This is about as question-begging as philosophy of language gets. Perhaps *that* is what Dennett wanted to demonstrate after all, i.e. just what-it-is-like to think like Dennett.

59

Doubts and Certainties

In *On Certainty* Wittgenstein writes:

> If you tried to doubt everything you would not get as far
> as doubting anything. The game of doubting itself
> presupposes certainty (Wittgenstein 1969: 115).

The notion of 'trying to doubt' something is a curious one, but perhaps one might try to find grounds for questioning the reliability of a particular piece bad news. Trying to doubt *everything* is even more curious. Why should one try to do that? In opposing doubt to certainty, Wittgenstein seems to be guilty of confusing logic with psychology. The logic of doubt makes doubt incompatible with certainty. *I am certain, but I doubt it* is a self-contradiction. Psychologically, however, the opposite of doubting as a mental act is not being certain but simply *not-doubting* (as distinct from *not being in doubt*).

English idiom is very misleading here. *I am in no doubt that P* is often used to indicate one's certainty that P. But there are many things we never doubt because we have never had occasion to consider them. There are many others that we never doubt because we do not understand enough about the subject to give them serious examination. For most of us, the sciences provide countless examples, i.e. of propositions which, in our lay ignorance, we are in no position either to accept or to doubt. We can always decide to take an expert's word for it. But this is at best certainty by proxy. We cannot make the expert's reasons our own.

So in between doubt and certainty lies this limbo or no-man's-land for which there is no convenient name. Its constant presence is overlooked or ignored by philosophers. Why? Because it offers no haven for the simplistic dichotomy which fascinates them – the age-old dichotomy between truth and falsehood.

60

Questions and Answers

According to Roderick Chisholm, 'Any inquiry must set out with *some* beliefs. If you had no beliefs at all, you could not even begin to inquire' (Chisholm 2000: 153). There are various ways of interpreting this claim. One leads to the uninteresting truism that in order to inquire you must believe that inquiry is possible. Other interpretations are more controversial. Does it mean that *any* beliefs whatsoever will suffice as the starting-point of inquiry? Or does it mean that you have to hold a belief in order to inquire into its credentials? That is less credible. One can examine the pros and cons of communism without being a communist. But what seems very likely is that the beliefs from which you start in any given line of inquiry will shape the scope of the ensuing investigation.

What are the minimum beliefs for linguistic inquiry? Some would place first a belief in the existence of languages, and next a belief that each language has its own community of users. These two are intimately connected, inasmuch as a language with no users (past or present) is taken to be tantamount to a contradiction in terms. It is usually assumed that the observable linguistic practices of this community offer the empirical evidence for studying the language in question. So in the absence of a body of speakers or writers, there is no language to investigate.

Matthews speaks blandly of 'a language in the ordinary sense, e.g. English or Japanese' (Matthews 2007: 215). But this so-called 'ordinary sense' is among the most questionable. The two examples Matthews offers are both languages with spoken and written forms, both languages including many varieties, and both having a long literary tradition. None of these features would seem to be criterial for the basic definition of 'a language'. No theorist can rule out *ex cathedra* languages which exist only in an oral form and lack a plurality of indigenous variations recognized as such by their speakers.

An integrationist would say that the minimum beliefs required for linguistic inquiry are (a) that it is possible to ask questions and (b) that to every question there is at least one possible answer. *Questions sponsor answers* or *Answers presuppose questions* are thus, on this view, alternative ways of formulating a fundamental principle of inquiry into human linguistic discourse. For whatever is said or written can form the subject of innumerable questions. We can ask who said or wrote it, to whom, when and why, etc. etc.

Questions and answers, nevertheless, are perhaps more complicated than most people realize. A question is not simply an interrogative sentence, and an answer is not simply a declarative sentence. The English sentence *Who are you?* is merely a metalinguistic abstraction. It is addressed to no one by nobody. It has no answer. In brief, sentences, unlike utterances, are not acts of speech. But the confusion between the two is one of the commonest mistakes in philosophy of language. The reason for this is that sentences may be both uttered and written. This causes students a great deal of perplexity, although it is actually no more perplexing than the fact that some debts may be paid either in cash or in kind.

In *How to do things with Words* J.L. Austin points out that a sentence as such is never a statement. But it can be '*used* in *making a statement*' (Austin 1965: 1fn. Italics in the original.) A question in the integrationist sense is certainly something less abstract than an interrogative sentence. It is a verbal move in a linguistic exchange, an item of discourse, an event both datable and locatable. The exchange is usually between two or more individuals. But a question may also be addressed to the questioner. (*Where did I leave my car keys? What is my doctor's telephone number?*) A question may or may not receive an answer. That depends on the circumstances. But its identity as a question presupposes the possibility of evoking a response of some kind.

The *adequacy* of an answer is a different matter, and depends on the question asked. So we might reformulate Chisholm's contention along the following lines. Our ability to ask and answer questions is part of our understanding of what it is to engage in verbal communication with others. This in turn requires believing in the co-existence of others as potential linguistic partners, i.e. as possible sources of questions and answers.

Unfortunately the matter is too complex to be left there, as the following passage indicates:

> While many would accept that language is an activity that must take place in a social setting, others have gone further by arguing that language is a social practice. This view commits one to the claim that the meanings of an individual's words are the meanings they have in the common language. (Smith 2000: 459)

An integrationist would certainly not wish to go this far. The notion of a 'common language' is part and parcel of the language myth of the Western tradition, upheld by many generations of grammarians. The professional grammarian claims to write grammars of English, French, Spanish, etc.; the concern in each case is with a fictitious or idealized collectivity of users, not with particular individuals. It is important to realize therefore that there is no such thing as *the* grammar of English, or any other language. Different grammarians adopt different systems of grammatical categorization. Thus, for example, Palmer declares unequivocally that 'English has no gender' (Palmer 1984: 195), whereas Quirk et al. in *A Grammar of Contemporary English* distinguish no less than ten genders (Quirk et al. 1974: 187). This blatant discrepancy tells us more about grammar and grammarians than pages of argument.

*   *   *

The mutual complementarity of question and answer is the fundamental mechanism of linguistic integration. It pervades the study of meaning in all its forms. For an utterance given as an answer to one question means something different if given as an answer to a different question. If there were *no* questions that one individual might ask another we should be living in a different world. And if questions could never be answered we should be living in a different world again. That is why the question–and–answer nexus is linguistically more basic in human society than phonemes, morphemes, words or alphabets. It provides linguistic roles for all the individuals who are members of a linguistic community. If you do not know how to ask a question or give an answer you do not understand the first thing about your own linguistic potential.

Recognizing question-and-answer as the basic linguistic mechanism is one way of avoiding an insidious trap to which many have fallen: trying to kick-start linguistic inquiry by defining a language. Attempts to define languages like English, French, Spanish, etc. invariably involve circularity. The language in question is defined by reference to a language-name (e.g. *English*) and the community of speakers and writers is identified with those who allegedly use the language with this name. In short, the language-names *English, French, Spanish*, etc. are treated as if they designated determinate languages or communities. But nothing could be further from reality. The linguistic divergences between members of one such community may be just as great as between one community and another. This is commonly disguised by the catch-all term *dialect*.

The criterion for distinguishing 'dialects' from 'languages' is usually said to be mutual intelligibility (Matthews 2007: 103). But as it stands this criterion is useless, because there may be varying degrees of mutual intelligibility within a linguistic community. The names of days of the week, for instance, may be used and understood by all; but not necessarily the vocabulary of specialist occupations (carpenters, locksmiths, sculptors, brewers, printers, etc.). Much depends on the size of the community and the social divisions within it.

What must strike an impartial observer as remarkable is how many theorists in the history of linguistics have opted to define *language* or *languages* in ways that beg the question instead of clarifying it. Here two illustrations will have to do duty for many.

1. William Dwight Whitney in *The Life and Growth of Language* declares that language comprises 'certain instrumentalities whereby men consciously and with intention represent their thought, to the end, chiefly, of making it known to other men: it is expression for the sake of communication' (Whitney 1875: 1). Here at least two terms, *thought* and *communication*, call for as much clarification as *language* itself; without it, the whole definition leaves Whitney's reader none the wiser.

2. Edward Sapir in his book *Language* describes language as 'a purely human and non-instinctive method of communicating ideas, emotions and desires by means of a system of voluntarily produced symbols' (Sapir 1921: 8). As compared with Whitney's account, this replaces 'thought' with 'ideas, emotions and desires', but retains the unexplained appeal to 'communication'.

These examples bear witness not so much to theoretical incompetence as to a certain kind of intellectual embarrassment. The embarrassment arises from having to explain to one's readers something with which they are already perfectly familiar, and *have to be in order to understand the explanation*. The 'solution' falls back in both cases on anchoring the definition to terms and concepts which – it is assumed – do not admit of further clarification. It is rather like the embarrassment of trying to explain verbally to a competent swimmer what swimming is. (No swimmer says gratefully: 'Oh, really? Is *that* what I was doing all along?)

In all human endeavours, experience takes priority over its verbal explanation. Every mistake in philosophy of language stems from ignoring or trying to reverse this relationship.

REFERENCES

Aristotle, *Nichomachean Ethics*. In J. Barnes (ed.), *The Complete Works of Aristotle. The Revised Oxford Translation*, Princeton, Princeton University Press, 1984.

Austin, J.L. (1961), *Philosophical Papers*, ed. J.O. Urmson and G.J. Warnock, Oxford, Clarendon.

Austin, J.L. (1962), *How to do Things with Words*, ed. J.O. Urmson, Oxford, Clarendon.

Benveniste, E. (1939). 'Nature du signe linguistique', *Acta Linguistica I*. Reprinted in *Problems in General Linguistics*, trans. M.E. Meek, University of Miami Press, 1971.

Benveniste, E. (1958), 'Catégories de pensée et catégories de langue', *Les Études Philosophiques 4*. Reprinted in *Problèmes de linguistique générale I*, Paris, Gallimard, 1966.

Bickerton, D. (2009), *Adam's Tongue*, New York, Hill & Wang.

Blackburn, S. (1996), *The Oxford Dictionary of Philosophy*, Oxford, Oxford University Press.

Bloomfield, L. (1923), Review of Saussure's *Cours de linguistique générale. Modern Language Journal*. Reprinted in C.F. Hockett (ed.), *A Leonard Bloomfield Anthology*, Abridged edn, Chicago, University of Chicago Press, 1987.

Bloomfield, L. (1935), *Language*, London, Allen & Unwin.

Campbell, L. and Mixco, M.J. (2007), *A Glossary of Historical Linguistics*, Edinburgh, Edinburgh University Press.

Chalker, S. and Weiner, E. (1994), *The Oxford Dictionary of English Grammar*, London, BCA.

Chisholm, R.M. (2000), 'Commonsensism'. In *Concise Routledge Encyclopedia of Philosophy*, London, Routledge, p.153.

Chomsky, A.N. (1968), *Language and Mind*, New York,
   Harcourt, Brace and World. 3rd edn 2006, Cambridge,
   Cambridge University Press.

Chomsky, A.N. (1986), *Knowledge of Language*, New York,
   Praeger.

Chomsky, A.N. (2000), *New Horizons in the Study of Mind*,
   Cambridge, Cambridge University Press.

Clark, U. (2007), *Studying Language*, Palgrave Macmillan.

Davidson, D. (1994), 'Davidson, Donald'. In S. Guttenplan (ed.),
   A Companion to the Philosophy of Mind, Oxford,
   Blackwell.

Dupré, J. (2009), 'Hard and East Questions about Consciousness'. In
   H-J. Glock and J. Hyman (eds), *Wittgenstein and Analytic
   Philosophy*, Oxford, Oxford University Press, pp.228-240.

Feser, E. (2006), *Philosophy of Mind*, Oxford, Oneworld.

Firth, J.R. (1957), *Papers in Linguistics 1934-1951*, Oxford,
   Oxford University Press.

Fodor, J.A. (1976), *The Language of Thought*, Hassocks, Harvester.

Fromkin, V. and Rodman, R. (1974), *An Introduction to
   Language*, 2nd edn, New York, Holt, Rinehart & Winston.

Gaukroger, S. (2012), *Objectivity*, Oxford, Oxford University
   Press

Harris, R. (1981), *The Language Myth*, London, Duckworth.

Harris, R. (1998), *Introduction to Integrational Linguistics*, Oxford,
   Pergamon.

Hawking, S. and Mlodinow, L. (2010), *The Grand Design*, London,
   Transworld.

Lycan, W.G. (2008), *Philosophy of Language*, 2nd edn, New York,
   Routledge.

Martin, R.M. (2010), *Epistemology. A Beginner's Guide*, Oxford,
   Oneworld.

Matthews, P.H. (2007), *The Concise Oxford Dictionary of
   Linguistics*, 2nd edn, Oxford, Oxford University Press.

Mautner, T. (ed.) (1997), *The Penguin Dictionary of
   Philosophy*, London, Penguin.

McGinn, C. (2004), *Consciousness and its Objects*, Oxford,
   Clarendon,

Mumford, S. (2012), *Metaphysics. A Very Short Introduction*, Oxford, Oxford University Press.

Nagel, T. (1974), 'What Is It Like to Be a Bat?', *The Philosophical Review*. Reprinted in D.R. Hofstadter and D.C. Dennett (eds.), *The Mind's I*, Harmondsworth, Penguin, 1982. Page references are to the reprint.

Palmer, F. (1984), *Grammar*, 2nd edn, Harmondsworth, Penguin.

Plato, *Theaetetus*. In J.M. Cooper (ed.), *Plato, Complete Works*, Indianapolis, Hackett, 1997.

Quirk, R. et al. (1974), *A Grammar of Contemporary English*, 5th impression corrected, London, Longman.

Reddy, M.J. (1979), 'The conduit metaphor – a case of frame conflict in our language about language'. In A. Ortony (ed.), *Metaphor and Thought*, Cambridge, Cambridge University Press.

Russell, B.A.W. (1940), *An Inquiry into Meaning and Truth*, London, Allen & Unwin. Page references are to the Pelican reprint of 1962.

Saussure, F. de (1922), *Cours de linguistique générale*, 2nd edn, Paris, Payot.

Smith, B.C. (2000), 'Language, Social Nature of'. In *Concise Routledge Encyclopedia of Philosophy*, London, Routledge, p.459.

Watson, J.B. (1924), *Behaviorism*, New York, People's Institute.

Wittgenstein, L. (1969), *On Certainty*, ed. G.E.M. Anscombe and G.H. von Wright, trans. D.Paul and G.E.M. Anscombe, Oxford, Blackwell.

Wittgenstein, L. (1978), *Remarks on the Foundations of Mathematics*, trans. G.E.M. Anscomble, 3rd edn, Oxford, Blackwell.

Wittgenstein, L. (2001), *Philosophical Investigations*, trans. G.E.M. Anscombe, 3rd edn, Oxford, Blackwell.